SOCCER BIOGRAPHIES

ERLING HAALAND

KENNY ABDO

Fly!
An Imprint of Abdo Zoom
abdobooks.com

abdobooks.com

Published by Abdo Zoom, a division of ABDO, P.O. Box 398166, Minneapolis, Minnesota 55439.

Printed in the United States of America, North Mankato, Minnesota.
052025
092025

THIS BOOK CONTAINS RECYCLED MATERIALS

Photo Credits: Alamy, AP Images, Getty Images, Icon Sportwire, Shutterstock
Production Contributors: Kenny Abdo, Jennie Forsberg, Grace Hansen
Design Contributors: Candice Keimig, Neil Klinepier, Victoria Bates

Library of Congress Control Number: 2024947816

Publisher's Cataloging-in-Publication Data

Names: Abdo, Kenny, author.
Title: Erling Haaland / by Kenny Abdo
Description: Minneapolis, Minnesota : Abdo Zoom, 2026 | Series: Soccer biographies | Includes online resources and index.
Identifiers: ISBN 9781098288846 (lib. bdg.) | ISBN 9781098289546 (ebook) | ISBN 9781098289898 (Read-to-me ebook)
Subjects: LCSH: Haaland, Erling, 2000---Juvenile literature. | Soccer players--Biography--Juvenile literature. | Professional athletes--Biography--Juvenile literature. | Manchester City Football Club--Juvenile literature.
Classification: DDC 796.334092--dc23

TABLE OF CONTENTS

ERLING HAALAND

Known as the Striking Viking, Erling Haaland has proven that scoring goals is in his field of expertise!

MANCHESTER
CITY
ETIHAD
AIRWAYS

EARLY YEARS

Haaland was born in 2000 in Leeds, England. His father was a local professional soccer player. The family then moved to Bryne, Norway. Haaland's love of sports grew. He enjoyed handball, track, and cross-country skiing. However, his main passion was soccer.

LEEDS CITY
MARKETS
DANIELS
Lebara
Lebara
Lebara
NOW OPEN
NEXT DOOR

hummel
Øster
Hus
OBOS
MASIV
MASIV
hummel
MASIV
0 3

Haaland joined the Bryne FK youth academy when he was five years old. Coaches noticed his skills quickly. Haaland joined Bryne's reserve team during the 2015–16 season. Just a year later, he moved up to the Bryne FK pro team at 16 years old!

GOING PRO

Haaland caught the attention of Molde FK in 2017. In 2018, he scored 12 goals in 25 matches. It was a season that earned Haaland an **Eliteserien** Breakthrough of the Year award!

sport 1
ekte sport.
sport 1
ekte sport.
19/6 1911
MFK

In 2019, Haaland joined FC Red Bull Salzburg. He helped Salzburg **clinch** the Austrian **Bundesliga**. The team also won the Austrian Cup. Haaland's skills during the **UEFA Champions League** was the talk of the town!

Haaland joined Borussia Dortmund in 2020. He scored 13 goals in 15 matches. The team also **clinched** a **Champions League** spot!

Haaland was awarded the **Golden Boy** award. It is an honor given to the best under-21 player in Europe!

During the 2020–21 season, Haaland scored ten goals. It made him the top scorer in the **UEFA Champions League**. Haaland also helped Dortmund win the **DFB-Pokal**. He was named **Bundesliga** Player of the Season.

By the 2021–22 season, Haaland had suffered injuries that limited his playing time. When he returned, he scored his 50th **Bundesliga** goal. Haaland was the youngest player to do so and he did it in the shortest amount of time!

ETIHAD
AIRWAYS

ETIHAD
AIRWAYS
CITY
CITY

In 2022, Haaland joined Manchester City. He was able to keep up his scoring ability with the new team. Haaland also broke multiple records during his first **Premier League** season.

Premier League

During the 2022–23 season, Haaland led the team to a **Premier League** title. Manchester also reached the **Champions League**!

MANCHESTER
FIFA
WORLD CHAMPIONS
2023
ETIHAD
AIRWAYS

During the 2023–24 season, Haaland became one of two players to have scored against every **Premier League** team he played. The following season, he matched Cristiano Ronaldo's record of scoring 100 goals for one team!

LEGACY

Off the pitch, Haaland uses his star status for good. In 2023, he gifted 175 boxes of soccer gear to children from his hometown of Bryne. More than 1,000 future soccer players felt encouraged by their hero!

Haaland's journey from a young talent to a superstar is filled with impressive awards and successes. As his career soars, Haaland will continue to strike a chord with fans!

ETIHAD
HAALAND
9

GLOSSARY

Bundesliga – Germany's top professional football league, consisting of 18 teams that play in a home-and-away format.

Champions League – a yearly soccer competition organized by the UEFA.

clinch – to confirm a win.

DFB-Pokal – an annual knockout competition organized by the German Football Association, featuring sixty-four teams.

Eliteserien – the top professional soccer league in Norway.

Golden Boy – an award presented by sports journalists to a young male soccer player in Europe who is considered the most impressive during the season. All nominees must be under 21 years old and play in the top tier of a European nation's league.

Premier League – the top level of the English Football (soccer) league system.

UEFA – short for Union of European Football Associations.

ONLINE RESOURCES

Booklinks
NONFICTION NETWORK
FREE! ONLINE NONFICTION RESOURCES

To learn more about Erling Haaland, please visit **abdobooklinks.com** or scan this QR code. These links are routinely monitored and updated to provide the most current information available.

INDEX